the boy on the beach

BY THE SAME AUTHOR

White Teacher

Wally's Stories

Boys and Girls: Superheroes in the Doll Corner

Mollie Is Three: Growing Up in School

Bad Guys Don't Have Birthdays: Fantasy Play at Four

The Boy Who Would Be a Helicopter

You Can't Say You Can't Play

Kwanzaa and Me: A Teacher's Story

The Girl with the Brown Crayon

The Kindness of Children

In Mrs. Tully's Room: A Childcare Portrait

A Child's Work: The Importance of Fantasy Play

vivian gussin paley

the boy on the beach

building community through play

THE UNIVERSITY OF CHICAGO PRESS

CHICAGO & LONDON

The University of Chicago Press, Chicago 60637
The University of Chicago Press, Ltd., London
© 2010 by The University of Chicago
All rights reserved. Published 2010.
Paperback edition 2014
Printed in the United States of America

23 22 21 20 19 18 17 16 15 14   3 4 5 6 7

ISBN-13: 978-0-226-64503-2 (cloth)
ISBN-13: 978-0-226-15095-6 (paper)
ISBN-13: 978-0-226-64505-6 (e-book)
10.7208/chicago/9780226645056.001.0001

Library of Congress Cataloging-in-Publication Data
    Paley, Vivian Gussin, 1929–
    The boy on the beach : building community through play /
    Vivian Gussin Paley.
        p.   cm.
    ISBN-13: 978-0-226-64503-2 (cloth : alk. paper)
    ISBN-10: 0-226-64503-7 (cloth : alk. paper)
    1. Play. 2. Early childhood education. 3. Fantasy games.
    I. Title.
    LB1139.35.P55P349 2010
    155.4'18—dc22

                                                    2009040626

To Irving

✳
✳

DEAR YU-CHING:

I have a name for us. We are anecdotists. The dictionary says this is someone who collects and tells little stories. Of course, our stories are all about young children, but I think the name fits.

DEAR VIVIAN:

Do anecdotists ask why? If so, then I agree to be called an anecdotist.

(Letters to and from Taiwan)

contents

preface

In his foreword to an earlier book of mine, *Mollie Is Three*, Michael Cole quotes novelist and physician Walker Percy, who comments,

> There is a secret about the scientific method which every scientist knows and takes as a matter of course.... The secret is this: Science cannot utter a single word about an individual molecule, thing, or creature in so far as it is an individual, but only in so far as it is like other individuals. (*The Message in the Bottle*)

My suspicion is that Walker Percy decided to write novels because he liked thinking about specific individuals who have stories of their own to tell, those characters who pop into a writer's mind and won't leave until they play out their urgent roles. Had Percy been a preschool or kindergarten teacher he would not have had to invent characters; the children would do this for him. He could have, as I describe on my first page, watched his people come and go, running, crawling, and strutting through the classroom, suggesting themes, confirming identities, and making claims until common ground is established: "I'm Superman and you're the lost princess, and I just found you because you're lost!" It is play, of course, and like a novel, it is more mystery than science.

We can approach the subject of play in more than one way. We can be guided by the aims and structures of "play scholarship," dealing with the theoretical, methodological, and ethical issues in rigorous, experimental ways, adding much of value to our knowledge of play. But I search for the meaning of play along more dramatic paths, trying to capture the shape of a scene before its image is blurred. The superheroes and lost princesses who play in the doll corner and block area refuse to be classified, charted, and diagnosed. "Let's pretend" turns us into storytellers and actors, on a stage where disguises are changed without notice, to suit every altered condition and impulse.

Do children make up their stories in order to play? Or do they play in order to put themselves into a story? Perhaps the secret lies in another direction. What if children play *and* invent stories because it is the way to distinguish themselves from all other individuals, even as they reach for common ground and community?

The boy on the beach seems to make up stories in order to both play and watch himself and others play. We, the observers, have a front row seat at the moment of creation.

the boy on the beach

1 ❊ the boy on the beach

The child at the shoreline cannot be more than four, but he is already an expert in staging a drama. Such concentration as his admits of few distractions; he barely notices when I stop to watch him. I wish I could bring a similar intensity to the manuscript I have left on my desk. Ironically, the boy and I share the same subject: he plays, and I write about play.

I want to know why children play as they do, and he owns part of the mystery. I have written a dozen books about young children, and I still cannot predict when the moment of supreme awareness will occur, for a child and for me, or how it will be played out.

A day in the kindergarten was for me like a chapter in a novel. Characters come and go, running, crawling, and strutting across the page, suggesting themes, confirming identities, and making claims until common ground is established. If I seemed at times to be manipulating the process, it was all in pursuit of having good conversations. Teacher or novelist, one wants to improve the narrative by fleshing out what is unspoken and overlooked as multiple plots converge. How far can we encourage the story while waiting for the perfect ending to come along?

My pen pal and fellow teacher Yu-ching and I have been writing to each other for several years, trying to pinpoint what is remarkable about the play we watch, but there are always more questions to ask. I so often have the feeling in a classroom that I am interrupting the play just as something important is about to be revealed. On the beach, however, time and tide favor the child's imagination, and there is seldom a reason to hurry the pace of the unfolding drama.

The boy on the beach has worked out a simple story. He uses two props, sand and water, and his stage directions are a series of sound effects with corresponding motions: "Pum, pum, pum" as he molds a sand house; "woo-ah-woo-ah" as he steers the fire engine; and "shwoosh-shwoosh-sh-sh" as he swings the hose in wide arcs. The mound of sand, the steering wheel, and the fireman's hose must perform their roles before the next wave arrives. The boy nods his head to denote each step in the process, and he frowns when his timing is off.

"All gone," he murmurs, surveying the damage. His pleasure is evident in the deep breath he takes, lifting his face to the sun. Several waves go by, and then he begins the procedure again. He sets aside a fragment of driftwood washed up on the sand.

"Put 'em here, okay?" the boy says to himself. Or does he speak to an invisible playmate? There seems always to be an inner monologue, explaining, motivating, questioning, and arguing, to enhance the mystery.

And yet why not just accept the activity at face value, as the simple pleasure of sand and water play, with a fireman's story to heighten the interest?

I can no more do this than justify my own purposes as merely "playing around." I want to be *on to something,* and so, I think, does the boy on the beach. He and I are both here to create metaphor and find hidden meanings in the moment. We are looking for the story that is ours alone to tell.

Watching the boy, I am certain he is involved in high drama. "Boy against nature," I'll call it: the waves tear down, and the boy rebuilds. Connections are made only to be broken apart and reestablished in new designs, with different characters dominating the scene. My mind races ahead, making up titles for what I see, as if the boy has submitted a manuscript to me for editing and chapter headings.

"Eli!" A woman's voice startles me. It is the boy's mother on a nearby blanket. "Honey, do you want some juice? Cover your eyes!" He shakes his head and pulls down his cap.

"Your son is very busy," I comment, and the mother laughs. "We forgot the sand toys," she tells me, "but, as you can see, it makes no difference. I wish his preschool teacher could see him. She told us he's too easily distracted, that he can't stick with anything. But we don't see that."

Eli glances at his mother, then at me, and I take advantage of the pause to speak to him. I would not have quizzed his mother about the book she is reading; it might appear intrusive. Yet it feels natural to discuss the fireman drama with her son. In the theater of the young, it is acceptable to ask the players to identify their characters and plots.

Their scripts are always in progress; ready to be revised and expanded when a new notion suddenly takes hold and shines its light into shadowy corners. It was in the same spirit that I questioned PhD students who did research in my classroom. Like the children, they were trying to establish their own interesting and provocative voices, eager to talk about what they hoped was a unique approach to an original proposal. Eli, of course, does not wonder whether his work is original. But he knows it is *his* work and must be given all his attention. The best questions about his work will come from other children; I serve as a pale substitute.

"You put out the fire," I note.

He nods vigorously. "Yeah, yeah, now it's gone. See, the water it's more stronger than the fire. It's not coming yet, the biggest wave. Ha! I see you!" He speaks directly to the waves, it seems. Their pace has slowed, and he has time to build a bigger house.

"Is that a second floor you're making?"

"Yeah, yeah, and a chimney!" Eli points to the driftwood at the top. "It's really tall, it's taller at that place. Oh-oh. Wah-wah, here it comes!" A new wave tumbles over the house, flattening it but not dislodging the chimney.

"You're dead, you're dead!" Eli jumps up and down, yelling at the waves, grabbing handfuls of wet sand and throwing them at the departing waves. "We gotcha now. You're busted!"

Eli's mother looks up sharply from her book. "Eli, what is going on?"

"I killed the monster," he tells her. "It hided in the waves. See, it was inside. You couldn't see it but I knew it!"

"Oh, good," his mother says, returning to her book. Triumphantly, Eli takes the driftwood and makes a large *E* in the sand, like an artist signing his work. Then, a moment later, he begins to dig a hole, scooping out the sand up to his elbows. He buries the driftwood, the letter *E*, and the remains of the house, with a sense of finality. I expect him to join his mother on the blanket and drink the juice she offered.

But the hole is a beginning, not an ending. Eli has the look of someone about to make up a new story. There were always children who looked this way when I rang the cleanup bell in my classroom. Luckily for Eli, there is no cleanup bell on the beach, nor does he have to collect his toys and straighten the shelves. Furthermore, like the adult researcher, he may make as many changes as needed to practice what he already knows and to imagine what the next steps might be.

I would like to stay and see what story comes after the fireman drama, but I must move on. Were Eli in my class, I could follow his daily dramas and make good conversation out of them. I might ask, "How did you know a monster was hiding in the waves?" It's a fair question, a sincere question, and only Eli has the answer.

What does it signify that a small boy invents a story never before heard or seen, exactly as he envisions it? He cannot mask his glee as he conquers the monster in the waves, but it is more than that. He seems to announce to himself: I, Eli, represented by the letter *E*, am someone with ideas; I am someone who turns ideas into actions, and actions into new ideas. Furthermore, I am intended to have my own ideas. That is why I play as I do, to show myself what my ideas are.

A graduate student once confided, "I can't tell if an experiment makes sense or is a dumb idea until I try it out with several groups of children. Even then, I need a few more rearrangements to get it to work." Eli would add, "And I need some explosions, too."

It is more than a decade since I've had my own classroom filled with characters looking for stories and stories looking for characters. Fortunately, the theatrical outpourings of the young are readily available wherever children play, and few places rank higher than a beach for observing the unlimited reach of a child's imagination. Eli is the surfer seeking the perfect wave, studying the highs and lows, not knowing in advance what the ultimate experience will be, but certain he will recognize it when it appears.

At the end of the beach, where the path enters an old pine and birch forest, I sit and watch the waves crash against the rocks. If Eli were here, he would don a superhero cape and fly above the waves in a daring feat of valor of his own choosing.

I once had a kindergartener named Eddie W. (there were two other Eddies in that class) who taped the letter *W* to his shirt and, like Eli, would pursue danger where the rest of us ignored the signals. His sudden rush into an ongoing activity often went unappreciated and mis-understood. If I could return to that time, I would be prepared with a better script. I might ask Eddie, "Who do you pretend to be when you crouch and pounce? Let's find out if this spaceship can use your character." These imaginary conversations are my own form of fan-tasy play, popping up especially when I walk alone on a beach or forest path.

Eli needs neither scribe nor negotiator. Children on a beach encounter few obstacles they cannot easily overcome. It is a different matter in a classroom. When my own room reached something like "the flow" de-scribed by psychologist Mihály Csíkszentmihályi, that sense of intense concentration Eli found at the beach, the children would call it a "nothing day." It was, for everyone, the best sort of day.

"Why a nothing day?" I asked when I first heard the term.

"Because nothing is happening."

"Do you mean that nothing much interrupts your play, that we have no place to go and no one is coming to see us?"

"Yes. Everything is just ordinary and just us."

An hour has gone by when I pass Eli again. He and his mother have been joined by an older woman with her granddaughter, perhaps, a girl of Eli's age. The women chat quietly on the blanket, punctuated by an occasional "Marianne, stay by the edge!"

It is clear that the plot has changed. The hole Eli was digging when I left has expanded into a series of holes, and at the bottom of the largest a small Lego doll lies in an inch of water. "Baby pool open!" Eli shouts. He is someone in charge, a lifeguard, or the man who cleans the pool. "More water!" he calls, and Marianne, the water carrier, pours it in. Pail in hand, she trudges back and forth, sloshing out most of the water before emptying the remaining cupful into the hole.

Eli keeps an eye on the waves. Suddenly, as if on cue, a big wave fills the hole. "She's drownding!" he yells gleefully, and Marianne reacts instantly. She pushes him aside, kneels down, and grabs her doll. "My baby!" she cries, touching the doll to her face. No more the silent water carrier, she is now Mother, in full command.

"Put her back!" Eli orders; then, in a more conciliatory manner, he pleads, "Can't she do the drownding for a tiny minute more?"

Marianne is stern. "No," she says, moving to an old mound of sand left over from Eli's fireman persona. Perhaps Eli should not have looked so pleased when the baby was in danger. Or maybe he was fooled by Marianne's initial cooperation in plans that were mostly of his making.

Marianne croons softly while she smooths the area for the baby's bed. "Go to sleep, Buttercup, go to sleep soon. When Daddy comes, mmm, go to sleep baby child, when Daddy comes, mmm."

Eli studies the scene, watching Marianne build up

the walls of the crib. To play or not to play is not his question. Of course he must play. Quickly he scoops up a scattering of little shells and fills the bottom of the pail. Holding an imaginary cell phone to his face he says, "I'm bringing home chicken nuggets, Mother. Look out the window. I'm in the SUV."

Eli and Marianne are a pair of dramatists, though often inclined toward different outcomes for individual scenes. But they both wish for stories that blend the familiar with the uncommon. As in a really good research study, play does not value closure. It seeks new direction and unexpected results. We want to be surprised but also reassured that we know the territory. The next wave may open a new vista, and we want to be prepared.

I feel more focused when I return to my desk. There are few events better than the play of four- and five-year-olds to release memories and stir up old connections for me. But I can never again be like the players on the beach. They take on new identities as easily as the roll of the waves. I cannot be the fireman who races to put out fires or the mother who saves her baby from drowning. Conventional thinking limits my own transformations, but once again I have glimpsed the nature and practice of being a child. As always, I sit in respectful wonder at the ultimate meaning and purpose of these dreamlike sequences.

If I am not a fireman or mommy to Buttercup, then perhaps I will be Lily Briscoe in Virginia Woolf's novel *To the Lighthouse*. She is the designated outsider, witness to the mysterious rituals of the family she studies, loving them yet unable to join them and be privy to their secret codes. Lily asks herself, "What is the meaning of life?" and finally, with relief, she decides

> The great revelation had never come. Instead there were little daily miracles, illuminations, matches struck in the dark . . . in the midst of chaos there was shape; this eternal passing and flowing was stuck into stability. "Life stand still here."

Is that the plan then? *Life stand still here*? If so, the children and I both want to watch these events carefully. The children must examine each scene in order to play in it, as must I, at a distance, in order to write down their words, to make what I can of them. It is an intimate connection we establish, the players and the observers. Together we watch the ways chaos finds a sensible shape. We marvel at the potential of the imagination to find its own questions and seek solutions, knowing that they are temporary and we can return in a new role the next day if we wish.

"To be continued" is our certainty and our comfort. We are not required to keep telling the same story or become stuck in any given role, but it is useful to experience its possibilities for a while.

My own story of Eli and Marianne unexpectedly continues when I discover them in a kindergarten I visit in the fall. I am delighted to realize that their dramatic renderings on the beach have been transferred to a new stage, and in a classroom that still preserves time for play. The first thing I do is write to Yu-ching in Taiwan, for she and I have already begun a conversation about the boy and girl on the beach, and there is nothing we like better than to follow a good classroom story.

2 ⁑ letters from taiwan

DEAR VIVIAN:

Your Eli and Marianne are like characters in a love story.
So I will give you another love story in return. You may call
it friendship, if you wish.

Yu-ching Huang is my pen pal. She teaches English to
young children in Taipei, and we have been writing to
each other since 2002, when I came to her classroom
to demonstrate my storytelling and story acting ideas.
It is a simple procedure, easy to copy. One by one the
children dictate stories to the teacher, who is scribe and
then stage director as the children act out the stories.

Our letters are nearly always about the children we
meet, their play and their stories; the subject holds end-
less fascination for us, and we try to write down the
children's exact words where we can. We like to describe
an episode of play, sometimes several of them, and then
speculate, interpret, or simply express amazement at
what children know without our telling them. Watching
young children play invites philosophical discourse, and
letter writing is the perfect place to try out our ideas. Yu-

ching admits she has become less interested in teaching English and more preoccupied with the narrative of children's play.

To me, it is all about friendship. The children are trying to find out how the pictures and words in their minds become the path to a friend. Even Eli, alone on the beach, has to imagine someone is playing with him until a real child comes along.

A boy in my class named Blanc, who is three, begins with a direct approach. "You are very beautiful," he tells Yu-shan. This happened two weeks ago, and he has already said it several times. Remember that most of the threes attend my school only once or twice a week.

A few days ago, sitting next to Yu-shan at storytime, Blanc told her again, "You are very beautiful." He kept staring at her, smiling, and repeating his compliment. Since Blanc had everyone's attention, I had to stop reading.

The book I was reading was about a little bear and his new baby brother. Shortly after, in the doll corner, Blanc told Yu-shan, "You are baby brother, and you are very beautiful. And I am beautiful bear too." Blanc makes them characters in a story, and now everything makes sense.

By the way, the children call Blanc the "you are beautiful" boy. To me, as I said, it is a love story. But when someone tells Blanc to dictate a "you are beautiful" story, he says instead, "The dragon is roaring." So I think that their play and the stories they dictate are not quite the same, are they? Maybe the story is more like a dream, and the roar of the dragon is an affectionate response to his friend Yu-shan.

15

I agree that these are love stories and friendship stories. "You are beautiful" must mean, "Will you be my friend?" Everything may be in code. When Marianne tells the doll, "Here's your daddy," perhaps she is saying, "You are my friend, Eli. I trust you to play with me." And I agree with you that a dragon's roar and a wolf's growl may have meanings we adults miss.

Your baby bear story reminds me of another more elaborate invention of a three-year-old named Aliza. She seems also to be trying to figure our how to use the baby bear character to express her feelings about someone new in her life, but in this case it's a baby brother. The incident does not take place in a doll corner, though it does seem to belong there. Maybe to a young child the whole world is a doll corner. Here is the play-by-play story:

Aliza sits down beside me on the carpeted steps in her grandparents' home. "Do you like Goldilocks?" she asks, smoothing her party dress. Her question is especially welcome, since I was about to mention her new baby brother, who is the center of attention in the living room.

"Yes. I do like Goldilocks," I tell her. "But I don't think she should go into the bears' house without being invited."

Aliza looks steadily at me, then turns her gaze to the closed door at the top of the stairs. "She thought her sister is sleeping. And she's hungry."

"I didn't know Goldilocks has a sister. Who is she?"

"Little Red Riding Hood. They got losted in the woods. And there's a wolf." Aliza bumps herself down the stairs

and returns a moment later with her doll. "I'm Goldilocks," she tells me.

"You're the friendly wolf," she decides quickly. "Because I cooked you some porridge." She cups her hands and holds them out to me. We sit there pretending to eat, and we watch the other guests congregating around the baby.

"And the baby comes," Aliza says.

"The baby bear?"

"The other baby bear. He lives there too."

Amazing, isn't it, Yu-ching? Blanc uses a baby bear to connect himself to Yu-shan, and in a different culture, across thousands of miles, Aliza finds a similar use for a baby bear as she thinks about a new baby brother. Apparently, from the earliest age there is a need to find characters to represent us if we are to contemplate serious issues.

By the way, I have a name for us. We are anecdotists. The dictionary says this is someone who collects and tells little stories. Of course, our stories are all about young children, but I think the name fits.

DEAR VIVIAN:

Do anecdotists ask why? If so, then I agree to be called an anecdotist. In Chinese, it would be "jiang ee she de ren," meaning people who tell stories not recorded.

Actually, I think the children are the anecdotists. Of course, their stories are very short, and they repeat them over and over, as if trying to understand a single thought. Ling pretends to be a bee, stinging people, stinging animals, stinging a flower, and so on. When she has had *enough of that, she moves on to butterflies. She is a butterfly on the flower, in the flower, on the lake, in the boat. Why? My answer is she wants to practice her thoughts, so she will understand better. She wants to see and hear her thoughts in action.*

Your Goldilocks girl also puts her thoughts into action, but a baby brother is more complicated than a bee. Even so, just from watching the other children, Ling decides to add babies to her own play. A boy drew a picture of five little circles surrounded by a big circle and told us they are baby frogs inside a mama frog. Spontaneously everyone got up and jumped around, finally jumping over to their own mothers, who sat against the wall. During the next playtime, Ling said she is the mother and everyone could be her babies. One story leads to another, I think, and the children play out the connections.

3 ❊ hurricanes
and howling wolves

Three months later, I come across Eli and Marianne again in Annie Olson's kindergarten. The school is not far from the beach where I first saw them play. The date is September 9, 2005, and the effects of Hurricane Katrina are being shown nightly on the television screen. In a few moments it will make landfall again, this time in the dramatic play of a group of children who live a thousand miles north of New Orleans.

The children in Mrs. Olson's room have never experienced a hurricane or seen floodwaters rise to cover the houses and farms they know. The waves that wash away their sand castles and the monsters hiding in the whitecaps do not match the pictures on the news of people and animals on rooftops and unidentifiable objects floating by. Mrs. Olson may be wondering how best to approach the subject, but the children cannot wait for her to take the lead. They are compelled to place these events into a recognizable context.

The five-year-olds in this room have been together

only a week, but they have no concerns about the sensitivity of the topics they choose to dramatize. Some of the children have known each other in preschool and played together on the beach, but the previous relationships tend to matter little when roles are identified. The story of the moment informs us of who the characters are and what they may say or do. The children begin the day in the manner of newscasters, announcing, "These are the fast-breaking stories we'll be working on today."

Eli and Marianne are in the doll corner when I arrive. As it happens, they are Mother and Father, as before on the beach, but this time they are waiting for Goldilocks. She is surely the all-purpose visitor whose ambiguous role makes her the perfect foil in domestic dramas. In this particular situation, before we can determine her influence, she becomes a character in a hurricane.

"Is the porridge ready?" Eli asks, setting the table while Marianne chooses a gown and stirs a pot. The scene is the equivalent of "Once upon a time." It will serve as the introduction for whatever is about to come. "Do you want blueberries, Dad? Goldilocks is picking blueberries for us in the forest."

"Yeah, yeah, and then the bears come and they don't know that . . . wait a minute." Eli stops in midthought and stares through the window over the stove. A pelting rain has begun, the wind blowing piles of leaves around in circles.

"Hey! Goldilocks is getting wet! She's drowning!" he says. "The water's coming in here. Hurry up, Mother, we got to get away." (Drowning? I will miss his "drownding," but this is what happens to most of our mispronunciations on the way to first grade.)

Marianne wraps her doll in a blanket and steps carefully around the table. "Is it wet over here? I think the wind is blowing on us."

At this point there is a dramatic turn in the plot and its stage business. Eli and Marianne change a domestic scene into a horror film. They begin to twirl blankets, pillows, dolls, and dress-ups in the air until the doll corner itself appears to be flying apart.

"Get on the roof!" Eli shouts, climbing on the table and pulling Marianne up with him. "Call 911! Call the Nationals! Don't miss the boat!"

He jumps off the table and stands on a chair. "The river is swimming up to here. Get inside my boat, Mother. The wolf is here too."

Marianne slips off the table and sits in the little rocking chair. "Is there a wolf, Eli?" she asks tentatively. The sudden appearance of a wolf causes her to step out of character. "Eli, are you still the dad?"

He understands her dilemma. "I'm the hunter dad, okay?" he says encouragingly. "I shot the wolf. But he's still huffing and howling. Can you hear him?"

"I'm the mother," she replies softly, barely rocking, as if she wants to slow down the action. Then, in a more confident voice, she says, "I hear him. I covered him with my blanket 'cause he's scared of the water. Are you still . . . are we still floating?"

Eli nods vigorously. "Yeah. Don't stand up in the boat.

I have to warn the people. The river is broken!" The inhabitants of a spaceship in the blocks already know they are in mortal danger. One of them shouts, "The hurricane is pouring on us!" As he speaks, he pushes over one side of the neatly stacked enclosure with a grand gesture. The hurricane is now official, and Mrs. Olson is alerted.

She is startled by the sudden increase in noise and activity. From her central location at the story table, she seems surrounded by children chanting, "The river is broke, the river is broke." Sal, at the nearby water table, is stirring up waves that are beginning to splash on the floor, and it is clear that the drama has invaded the room. It occurs to me that I have seldom seen so universal a response to a drama that started in the doll corner.

Mrs. Olson is on her feet, prepared to act. She rings her little bell—her magic wand, we might say—with more energy than usual. The bell fulfills her own fantasies of control over nature. The mess is huge, but she does not appear worried. Perhaps her years of experience inform her that she is observing a dramatic performance and not random mayhem. Maybe the fact that she grew up with four brothers, which I heard her tell the children once as she described one of their escapades, has made her more sympathetic to sudden explosions. In any case, the creative approach she uses to calm the waters surprises me.

"The National Guard is here!" she calls out in a firm but kindly voice. "Pretend we're the National Guard. Watch me put on my uniform. I'm pulling on my hip boots. Let me see everyone pull on your hip boots. And my yellow rain slicker. Put yours on too. There's no time to lose."

Mrs. Olson is determined to treat the children as actors, not outlaws, and she will join them in the performance. She is doing what Marianne did for Eli on the beach, giving him a new script to follow. "Okay, boots on? Now, we count to twenty so the water can go down. Then we'll clean up all the streets and houses in New Orleans."

"One, two, three, four . . ." the children begin, in a somber mood, watching the imaginary floodwaters recede. It is only the fourth day of school, but the children in Mrs. Olson's room are already bound together in the new literature they are producing with the assistance of a teacher who takes their invented plots and characters as seriously as those she finds in books.

When she says, "Pretend we're the National Guard," she knows she has the attention of every child. She understands that make-believe is the children's subject and has been since before they took their first steps. There are teacher guides for math and science, but none for pretend hurricanes and howling wolves—or for drowning dolls and visits from Goldilocks and her sister.

Just as Eli and Marianne did in the case of an errant wave, Mrs. Olson and her classroom of children must create their own guides for each incident as it happens. They share a similar goal: to reach a level of mutual awareness, and to find the words and actions to satisfy the actors on the stage and the audience in the arena.

Virginia Woolf has another way of describing the

Insight

process. She is concerned with writers and their readers, but if we substitute "children" and "playmates" for writers and readers, we can easily adapt her words from a 1924 essay called "Mr. Bennett and Mrs. Brown."

> The writer must get in touch with his reader by putting before him something he recognizes, which therefore stimulates his imagination and makes him willing to cooperate in the far more difficult business of intimacy. And it is of the highest importance that this common meeting place should be reached easily, almost instinctively, in the dark, with one's eyes shut.

Watching Annie Olson pull on imaginary hip boots, it becomes clear to me that the quotation applies equally well to teachers: the *teacher* must get in touch with the children by putting before them something they recognize, which therefore stimulates their imaginations and makes them willing to cooperate in the business of intimacy.

This is the task of the anecdotist as well, whether teacher or child. We want to be able to one day say, "Remember the time when we played hurricane, and we were the National Guard and wore our hip boots so we could stand in the deep waters and clean up the city?"

4 : letters

I ask myself every day, why do young children make up these characters and plots, one after another? It doesn't matter if they come from fairy tales or TV; the children use them in private ways. Right now, this is what I think: children become a character who is not themselves in order to prove the necessity of their existence.

It sounds logical to me in Chinese, but I am not sure how it sounds in English, so let me explain further. When they solve one problem, they create another to act on. By proving they are necessary and useful in a story, they demonstrate that they have a reason to exist, to be here with others. Even your Eli playing alone on the beach is pretending there are other characters in his story. And Aliza, playing with you, has to show she is necessary to the baby brother. She can't do this yet by being herself because she is unsure of what it means to be a sister. But she can imagine Goldilocks and Little Red Riding Hood as sisters, and she can imagine a baby bear living with them in the bears' house.

Here is an example from my morning group that shows how children will make up a character in order to find a use for themselves in a group. Three girls, all age three, have just come to school for the first time. They cling to their moms and refuse to join us for any activity, not even at book time, when I am most likely to use a few English words.

After one mother has given up trying to persuade her child, the little girl gets down and crawls away, meowing and purring, into the doll corner. I call out, "Who are you?" and she answers, "Kitty."

"Is kitty hungry?" I ask.

"Is buying grocery."

All this is in Chinese, of course. I don't want to make play an excuse for lessons. Now the second girl crawls and me-ows after the first, which is interesting because they do not know each other. In a moment, the third girl does the same.

They are all in the doll corner, meowing at each other and licking their paws. The girls now are friends, as easy as that. They have proved they are necessary to each other and to all the children who are smiling at them and begin-ning to meow with great pleasure.

DEAR YU-CHING:

I repeated your kitten anecdote to a group of teachers and asked, "Why do the girls dare to leave their mothers only when they can pretend to be someone else?" One teacher said, "If you are afraid then you pretend to be someone who is not afraid." Another teacher thought you might pretend to be someone who is afraid, such as a crying baby in a crib. Most of the teachers would agree with you that the little girls do not know what a child is supposed to do in a classroom, but they can easily imagine what a kitten does in a doll corner.

I have my own kitten (and puppy) story for you that involves older children as well. The scene is a suburban library where I have been invited to demonstrate story dictation and acting to parents, teachers, and librarians, as we did at Play Space in Taipei six years ago. (So long ago!)

A group of children, ages three to seven, most of whom did not know one another, had been assembled to help me demonstrate the activity. I began in the same way as in your school, marking off a stage with masking tape and using a story I'd brought with me. Of course, we didn't need you to be our translator, but everything else was quite the same.

Anyway, most of the children in the library got the idea right away, but the two youngest, a boy and girl of perhaps three or four, would not participate. However, when I ask, "Who will be the cat?" in an older child's story, the little girl hops down from her mother's lap and begins to meow and crawl to the stage. Then the boy begins to bark, and he follows the girl as if they are old pals. The boy woofs his way to the stage and keeps barking. When I point out that there is no dog in the story, he barks louder. Thereafter, the cat and dog insist on being in every story. This being the case, of necessity, each new story has a cat and dog written into it.

Later, several parents ask me why I allowed the two children to interfere with the stories, and I remind them that I took my cue from the older members of the group. They did not object to their stories' being changed. They seemed curious about the behavior of the youngest children and did not find the cat and dog unwelcome additions. On the contrary, the two little ones made the dramas appear more personal and intimate, like play itself. It was as if we were all at home—or on the beach—where the rules are relaxed and you can run into a wave or dig a hole, following the impulse of the moment.

It seems to me now that the children in the library were demonstrating something to me that I had not been anticipating: a further application of the Virginia Woolf quotation. The two youngest children did not recognize the activity I was presenting, which made them unwilling to cooperate. The older children understood their problem immediately and, by inserting cat and dog characters, allowed them to reach a common meeting place with the group, instinctively and intimately.

DEAR VIVIAN:

Your library story echoes my thought that children become pretend characters in order to be necessary to other children. The older children made good use of the cat and dog as a reason for their stories. I think the activity became more interesting and easier thanks to the presence of little children who wouldn't play by the rules.

Didn't the same thing happen in your book, "The Boy Who Would Be a Helicopter," when Jason insists on being a helicopter in every story? Most adults would consider this an obstacle to creativity, but as it turned out, the children happily adapted to the situation and became more creative and uninhibited.

DEAR YU-CHING:

Another thought about our kitty and helicopter boy anecdotes: Are the children simply being kind to those whose behavior is out of step? To go further, are these demanding classmates giving us the opportunity to be kind? "Creative kindness," we could call it, an outcome easier to manage in a dramatic scene where we can change our stories and insert new roles to suit the needs of classmates who require help.

DEAR VIVIAN:

"Creative kindness" is good. To let someone be necessary is creative kindness. We make up a story in which kindness is like a character that must be given words to say. When Mrs. Olson put on hip boots and gave the children an honorable way to clean up the mess, she was being creative and kind. She provided their story with a good ending.

5 : a lonely wolf

When Eli dictates his wolf story to Mrs. Olson, I decide to stay for lunch and perhaps find out more about wolves and waves. This is Eli's story: "The wolf turned the boat over when a big wave comes. Everyone has to swim fast to the other boat."

Mrs. Olson asks for more information. "Did the wolf do it on purpose? Was it an accident?"

"Yeah, a accident. He wasn't never on a boat before so he doesn't know how to sit still."

At lunch I bring up the subject again. "Eli, when the wolf in your story turned over the boat, was he worried because the boat was going up and down on the waves?"

"Yeah, yeah, that's why. He was even seein' could he get out of there."

"'Cause he doesn't know how to swim?" Julia asks. "Does a wolf know how to swim?"

"Yeah, remember in the gingerbread boy?"

"No, Eli, that was a fox," George corrects him.

"Oh, yeah, a fox. Anyway this wolf doesn't swim. And everyone else is swimming away. So he's just looking at them. And they're not looking at him." Eli's description goes right to the heart of the matter; someone is in trouble, and no one pays attention.

Julia says, "The wolf is lonely. They hafta give him a long pole to grab. They're supposed to pull him if he can't swim. He is huffing too much, Eli."

"No, he stopped huffing," Eli assures her. "You don't go scarin' people if it's a hurricane."

"So, that's it," Julia worries. "They left him alone."

The children's sympathy toward the wolf surprises me. "You all seem sorry for the wolf," I comment. "Isn't this the same wolf who scares the three pigs so much? They certainly don't like him, do they?"

Marianne has been listening to the conversation while finishing her yogurt and banana. "But if nobody doesn't like you then you're sad," she says. "And lonely." She looks at Julia, acknowledging "lonely" as Julia's word. "But that wolf could still be a bad guy," she concludes. "Right, Eli?"

Eli gets up and walks around the table, jelly sandwich in hand. "Yeah, yeah, but so what? See, everyone thinks the wolf is mean, but really he's not."

"Even if he bothers the little pigs and blows down their houses?" The children accept my devil's advocate stance, but they all look at Eli for a resolution to the uncertainty.

"No!" he states firmly. "First everyone has to stop thinking the wolf is mean and act nicer to him."

These children have reached a place of intimacy with the wolf. They know he is considered a bad guy, but they have played with him and even taken his role, or that of other characters who disrupt and disobey. And they know a boy named Stanley.

"Don't talk no more about this," Noah urges. "'Cause Stanley isn't here."

"And if Stanley isn't here?" I ask.

"Because he growls at us, and he's a wolf sometimes too."

"So he'll want to hear this conversation?"

"He's our friend."

I join the table cleaners, and Mrs. Olson whispers to me, "Come back tomorrow and meet Stanley. You can judge for yourself."

I wonder if Stanley will turn out to be like a boy named Daryl whom I met in a Chicago preschool a few years ago. His teacher had warned me that Daryl roars during playtime, telling children he's going to eat them. However, when he dictates a wolf story to her she can see how vulnerable his wolf character is.

"A wolf story," Daryl begins. "The bad wolf is on the roof. He falled off because he was scared. He was scared because he hurted himself. And the pigs went on a walk on a rainy day."

"The pigs pay no attention to the wolf lying on the ground hurt?" the teacher asks. "They just go off on a walk?"

"They don't care," Daryl explains. "'Cause they wasn't being hurt."

6 ❋ letters

DEAR YU-CHING:

Did you ever wonder if the children (and we as well) make up characters and plots just to pass the time in an interesting way? I thought of this when I came upon the following idea in The Magic Mountain, a very long novel by Thomas Mann.

"We tell a story in order to give meaning to time, since time has no shape or essence itself."

Shortly after reading this, I came upon a good example of Mann's words in, of all places, my local post office. I am in a long line of impatient customers waiting for service at the only open counter. Two sisters, ages three and five perhaps, are seated together in a stroller, oblivious to the scene around them. They seem to be practicing the beginning of a mermaid story, giving "meaning to time" for them and also for me.

"Pretend we're mermaids," says the older sister. "And you didn't learn how to swim yet. Say that."

"You didn't . . ."

"No, you hafta say I didn't."

"I didn't."

"... didn't learn..."

"... didn't learn..."

"... to swim yet."

"... swim yet."

"Good. Now I say—pretend I say—I'll teach you how. I'll teach you how."

"Okay, pretend."

"Because pretend I'm the big sister mermaid that knows how. Move your arms this way."

"Okay, pretend."

Is this a grammar lesson disguised as pretend play? Or is it basically one of your love stories? Indeed, there is such an intimate feeling created as one sister initiates the other into the art of fantasy that I cannot look away. I felt the same way sitting on the staircase with Aliza when she named me the friendly wolf. These children not only give meaning to time but new dimensions to space as well. The sisters prepare to swim along the ocean floor, and Aliza and I sit in the middle of a forest.

DEAR VIVIAN:

My mind is jumping around trying to figure out everything the older mermaid sister is doing. She is thinking about her roles as sister and mermaid, as a teacher and a dramatist, and as the storyteller who is filling time and space. Maybe she is also being her mother's helper, keeping her little sister from becoming bored and restless. It amazes me how much these little children already know and are thinking about while I interrupt them to teach them something.

They fool us by being so changeable. For example,

Chwan upsets the girls when he is a terrible dragon, but he can instantly become the gentle grandfather, the boss of the riverboat, or the one who calls out English words when I ask for them. And he still has room left in his head to tell me that Peter Rabbit is his baby brother who runs away and is lost forever. I guess Chwan has a lot on his mind besides my lessons.

7 : stanley is here

When I arrive in Mrs. Olson's room, there are no signs of yesterday's hurricane. A huge event of that sort is seldom repeated. If the question being asked was, "What would happen if we were struck by a hurricane?" Eli and the others may have found some answers. To the observer it looked like the impulse of the moment carried to its fullest extremes, for the sheer exuberance of throwing things around. And yet the end result was the model of a well-organized cleanup, and sensitive connections were made between the attempt to rescue a wolf and a boy named Stanley who apparently sometimes impersonates a wolf.

I survey the room as I await Stanley's arrival. The scene in the doll corner is as far from the center of a storm as one could imagine, except for the clothing littering the floor, chairs, and cribs. Marianne and Sarabeth are trying on dresses, hats, and scarves in front of a long mirror. The mess is great, but the mood is serene.

"How do I look?" Marianne asks.

"You are the prettiest princess," says Sarabeth. "How do *I* look?"

"Now you are the prettiest, prettiest princess. How do *I* look?"

"You are the prettiest, prettiest, prettiest princess," and so on. The simple call and response continues even as the girls, dressed to the nines, move over to a coloring table, where other girls pick up the refrain. "Prettiest, prettiest, prettiest, prettiest."

Mrs. Olson passes by and whispers, "We could use another hurricane about now. I'd say the girls needed to reestablish the female code."

We both laugh. "Was the hurricane a male code, then?" I ask.

"Absolutely. The girls went along with it, but it's a boy thing entirely."

In the block area, another "boy thing" is going on. Eli and three other boys are playing "poison machine," a label repeated nearly as often as "prettiest princess." Their play involves enemies, hidden or dead, and a sizable collection of weaponry made of cardboard tubes joined with masking tape. The poison machine explodes each bomb as it is tossed up, and the boys, in unison, yell "Kaboom!" and other loud noises. Then the numbers of dead and wounded are tabulated.

"Six dead."

"Eight dead."

"Twenty wounded."

"Woo-ah-woo-ah!" I recognize Eli's siren, the same one used on the beach for a fire engine, and now equally appropriate for the approaching ambulance.

Mrs. Olson has invited me to be the story teacher, the

person who takes down the children's dictation during playtime and helps them act out their stories later in the morning. "It will keep you occupied while you wait for Stanley," she jokes.

Eli is first on the story list and comes quickly when I call him, though he keeps looking at the action on the rug. He rattles off his story, sitting on the edge of the chair. "The enemy has ten hundred explosives but we got the bomb catchers and they don't. Everyone bad dies. The end."

"No wounded, Eli?" I ask. "Over there on the rug you have wounded fighters. That's why I'm wondering." He smiles at my question. "Oh, yeah, these guys don't come alive, that's why. If you're wounded, you come alive." He is gone before I can find out if he wants that explanation written into his story. In any case, Julie, next on the list, is already seated beside me.

"I was a bad guy once and I died," she tells me.

"How was it?"

"Okay," she says, and then begins her story. "There was a princess and a baby bear and they hided behind a tree. And a friendly wolf comes. And the sun comes up. And the princess and the baby bear eat breakfast in the wolf's cave. They were friends." Julie turns to the door. "Stanley is here," she notifies me, as if his arrival is part of her story.

From the moment Stanley enters the room, it is clear that he is different from the other children. Mrs. Olson walks to the door quickly and greets him warmly, but she does not stop watching him until, after what seems to be a highly ritualized fast walk around the room, he settles into the doll corner, where Marianne and Sarabeth have returned to change costumes.

It is indeed Stanley the wolf, filling the room with soft growls and murmurs. He zigzags through the play areas as if he is alone in a maze, giving everyone and everything a light tap but looking at no one. Finally he collapses into the little rocking chair in the doll corner, pulling his jacket over his head.

"Here's baby brother!" Marianne says sweetly. "Or do you rather to be Dad?" There is no response from Stanley, nor do the girls seem to expect one. But when Sarabeth says, "Look, Stanley, we're butterfly sisters," he uncovers his head and looks directly at the girls. They spread their wings and tiptoe around his chair.

"Who do you want to be?" they persist, beginning a comforting hum. "Who uh who uh who la la."

"How 'bout a butterfly dad? That's a good one," Marianne assures him.

"I'm Stinger-Ray Wolf," Stanley says, his first clear, face-to-face communication.

"Is he a dad?" both girls ask.

"A dad. Yeah."

The girls clap their hands. For the moment at least, Stanley has found his role. It is the perfect wave on a day at the beach, and Mrs. Olson senses the magic. She extends playtime so that everyone can benefit. The butterfly sisters are bringing Stinger-Ray Wolf-Dad his supper, and in the blocks an alien ship arrives with treasures stolen from the pirates of Bloody Swamp.

Mrs. Olson fixes us a cup of Earl Grey tea, and we decide to sit back and watch the children play. I am reminded of my first teaching position in a New Orleans nursery school almost sixty years earlier. At 10:30 every morning, the housekeeper came by with a tray of café au lait, strong coffee with hot milk. She would always tell the children, "Now ya'll play real good for a while so your teachers can enjoy their coffee." It was the best time of the morning for all of us.

interesting insight

8 ⁑ letters

DEAR VIVIAN:

With "prettiest princesses" and "poison machines," the children understand each other so well, don't they? They keep practicing just to see what will come of it, but they always get the point. Sometimes, however, there are ordinary phrases or concepts that we adults take for granted but the children are mystified.

Now, we have a custom you don't have, of addressing teachers by their last names followed by the title "Teacher." So you would be Paley Teacher, for example. Here is a five-year-old girl, I-Ting, who is smart as can be but misses the point of this common structure.

We were chatting one day while she ate some cookies and I drank my coffee. She was telling me about her "real" school (she comes to me only for English lessons) and about her two teachers.

"What are their names?" I asked.

"One is Zheng and the other is Fong," she said.

"Oh, then, they are Zheng Teacher and Fong Teacher," I commented.

I-Ting was startled. "How do you know?" she asked. I

was even more surprised, and I said, "It's you who told me their names." She thought for a moment and said, "You must be very smart."

Let me explain: since we always put last names before first names, (I am Huang Yu-ching) I-Ting must have thought "teacher" was their first name. After a few other topics, we came back to "teacher" again. This time she told me her music teacher is Yo.

"Then she is Yo Teacher," I said carefully.

"How do you know that too? You must be very smart," she said again. Inside of me, I was laughing very hard. One day it will all become clear to her, but meanwhile look how she needs to practice the concept with all her teachers. Until then, she will tell me how smart I am.

DEAR YU-CHING:

We can understand I-Ting's confusion. Any child could make the same error. But they would not be confused by a boy named Stanley in Mrs. Olson's class even though the adults are stymied by his behavior. When he comes into a room he cannot settle down until he has traced a path through every activity, touching every child, toy, and piece of furniture. Yet the children do not ask, Why does Stanley do this? Why does Stanley growl like a wolf? They simply say, This is who Stanley is, and he is our friend. Certainly it is one of your love stories, but it is also a story of community. Children like Stanley reveal much about what is being built in a classroom besides castles and spaceships.

P.S. I'll be visiting other schools for a while, right in the middle of Stanley's story, it seems. But I will return.

9 ∗ baby unicorns
and glue fairies

My first stop is in a kindergarten outside Boston, where playtime has just begun. "I'm a baby unicorn," Angela says, putting on a sequined cap and vest. If one function of play is to create scenes to remember and talk about, then Angela's opening statement sets the stage effectively. The unicorn is a promising character because, as with Goldilocks, there are few preconceived limitations.

"Do you fly?" asks Naomi, newly arrived and eager to locate the pink tutu before someone else does. "Are you a flying unicorn?"

The question surprises Angela, who looks at her arms and frowns. "Where's my feathers? I need my feathers to fly."

The girls are off to a good start, on their way to a common meeting place that can be reached easily and explored for its dramatic and social possibilities. Naomi chooses a worrisome tack: "Maybe baby unicorns doesn't fly yet," she says, picking through the dress-ups until she finds the only article of clothing that will identify her as Pink Fairy. She seems not to notice Angela's disappointed look, but Michael, nearby, sees her predicament.

He is struggling to complete his own necessary wardrobe, for he is a superhero whose cape will not stay tied. "Yeah, you could fly," he says. "I only hasta dig you some feathers. But first I gotta get on this cape."

Naomi repositions herself. "Oh, if you got feathers! I didn't hear about that. Sure you could fly. Make it I'm Pink Fairy who is also Glue Fairy. I'll glue them on, okay?"

"Do it here, here, and here," Angela says, holding out her arms, but Naomi injects another suspenseful note. "Uh-oh, I just lost my power!"

How easily the drama unfolds. The actors move from frame to frame, assessing character and plot, adding costume and dialogue, bringing the action forward in little increments, savoring each moment of doubt or joy. "I'll call the Queen Fairy," Naomi says, holding her hand to her face, as with a cell phone.

"Hello, Queen Fairy? I need my power back. Okay? Okay, she gave it back to me. I got my power."

"Wait!" Michael calls out. The teacher has fastened his cape, and his arms are stretched before him in superhero style. "There's a guy trying to steal your feathers! Psh-sh-t-t-t! I froze him with my x-70 ultra charge ray gun!"

Naomi pushes his arms away. "No, I'm the Pink Fairy! I got my power. Not you!"

"Watch out, Pink Fairy, don't take a step. Stand there. Don't move! I gotta wipe away the ultra rays. Or you'll freeze!"

The teacher's bell rings. "We didn't play yet!" Angela whines, but the children are not too dismayed. The impasse between Pink Fairy and Superman can be resolved later; every interrupted story will be remembered and reinstated at the next opportunity. Perhaps Baby Unicorn will begin a new episode with her feathers intact, ready to fly.

A contemporary Hasidic storyteller, Rabbi Shlomo Carlebach, contrasts teaching and storytelling. "In teaching," he said, "we are to learn what we do not know. But of a story, we ask, 'Let me know what I know.'"

And so it is with young children who play in order to see what they already know and what they might wish to experience again in a different way. "There was a pink fairy," Naomi dictates later in the morning. "And she loses her powers. And she can't fly. The end."

"She doesn't find her powers again?" I prompt.

Naomi considers the options. "No, Pink Fairy doesn't get her powers back."

I feel disappointed, though a scribe should maintain a degree of impartiality. Yet I want the children's stories to end on a happy note, even knowing that this does not always create the best make-believe. It may be necessary to undergo helplessness and sadness on occasion, if only to be able to introduce a new scene in which to exclaim, "I can fly again! My powers are back!"

"I wonder if Pink Fairy will get back her powers," I ask Naomi. "In your story."

"Maybe tomorrow," she reassures me. "Fairies are magic, you know."

Naomi knows that it is she who gives Pink Fairy her power. And Eli certainly knew that it was *he* who put the monster in the waves. As good anecdotists, they are always looking for ways to improve their stories. This being the case, the task of the teacher becomes easier. We pull on our hip boots and call on the National Guard when the outcome seems too chancy. The teacher who tells stories is in a position to help children make connections and pull a storyline along to the next level.

10 : bad stuff

"In the midst of chaos there was shape" could be the title of the scene I come upon during my next school visit, to a bilingual preschool in Connecticut, where four-year-old Emily sits alone in the block area smashing two rubber dinosaurs into each other with unusual vigor.

Hers is the sort of behavior that often causes the observer to say, "That child doesn't know how to play." The assessment would be wrong, as we are all to discover, for the action in the blocks is a prelude to an important and unexpected lesson.

I hesitate to approach her. Normally I might ask, "Would you like to tell me a story about the dinosaurs? Then we can act it out later with the other children." But Emily's play discourages such ordinary discourse. Fortunately, Emily sees me watching her and brings her dinosaurs to me.

She holds one up and says something in Spanish, switching to English when she sees I do not understand. "This kid dinosaur is dancing," she tells me. "And the baby one is flying. But they isn't friends. They got to fight every time." She emphasizes her narrative with a few more smacks, head to head.

"May I write down what you said?" I ask.

"Why?" she wants to know, looking curiously at my notebook.

"Because I like to collect stories. Here, listen: 'This kid dinosaur is dancing. And the baby one is flying. But they isn't friends. They got to fight every time.' There. Now we can act it out soon."

"Which one says dinosaur?" Emily puts a finger on the page and I place it on the word. "It has a *d*," she says, "like daddy."

"Do you want me to write down why they are fighting?"

"Bad stuff. The kid dinosaur eats bad stuff, bad stuff. With his big ugly mouth. He can't do that. The baby don't never eat that bad stuff." When I ask what the bad stuff is she smiles. "You know, all that bad stuff?"

"Okay. Now, when we act out your story, who will you be—the kid or the baby dinosaur?"

She laughs out loud. "Oh, I'm the kid dinosaur, for sure. I eat, eat, eat all the bad stuff."

Emily's story will serve as our demonstration, though I wonder if the teachers will be uncomfortable with all the fighting. However, as the action begins, with Nora as the baby dinosaur and Emily pretending to gulp down the bad stuff, the children and teachers express their delight and surprise. Emily's little drama is recognizable to everyone but me.

"I'm not your friend! Bad stuff, bad stuff!" is taken up

by the entire group. "Bad stuff, bad stuff!" I feel I have walked into someone else's dream.

When the children go out to the playground, I ask Emily's teacher if she can help me understand the dinosaur story. "Sorry," she replies. "I should have explained. See, it's really all about Emily's mom, a peculiar situation. She is incredibly offended, angry really, when parents take their children to McDonald's instead of cooking good food at home. Especially her Mexican neighbors, some who have children in our center. She'll yell at them in Spanish, and it's not pleasant, let me tell you."

"I'm beginning to understand. And Emily copies her mom?"

"You bet. Frankly, it's a big problem for us. This little story brought us all a great sense of relief. We could all yell, 'Bad stuff, bad stuff!' together. It was exhilarating, really."

"Yes, I could see that. Were you surprised that she made herself the bad one?"

"Only at first. But then it seemed the natural thing to do, for her to finally be the one who eats the bad stuff, which is to say, the ordinary child, not the vigilante. We've been talking to her, trying to get her to see the other child's point of view, but to no avail. And now she herself literally steps into the other child's role and has everyone yell at *her*."

"Will you show the story to Emily's mother?" I ask.

"Absolutely. Emily has come up with a remarkable way of trying to come to terms with a social conflict, and her family should be proud of her. This will not be hard for them to understand. Her family loves folktales and stories from their childhood. Emily's story has all the elements of a folktale, don't you think?"

I *do* think so. Emily, with her battling dinosaurs, has created a curriculum with which to study the subjects of exclusion, loyalty to family standards, and notions of public morality, topics often found behind the scenes in folktales and family stories. When we are young we need the dramatic impulses of play to help us organize such complex ideas, to put a face to them and watch characters play them out in familiar ways.

"And to think," says Emily's teacher as we say good-bye. "We would never have known why the dinosaurs were clobbering each other without the storytelling activity."

"It's difficult to know if this is true," I admit. "Don't forget, Emily was already explaining the conflict to *herself* as she played. Maybe what the dictated story does is explain it to everyone else, and she might have found other ways to do this, once she clarified the matter for herself. However, putting a scene up on a stage for everyone to examine together makes it easier. I will never forget all of you yelling out 'bad stuff, bad stuff' so joyfully. *That* explained a lot to me about the power of theater."

When I return from Connecticut there is a letter waiting from Annie Olson:

DEAR VIVIAN:

I hope, after your travels are over, you won't forget to come home to our classroom. We share so many stories together, it feels like you are a part of the family. And I have a new Stanley piece for you–a piece of the puzzle.

This morning, as Marianne was getting ready to dictate a story, she said, "Stanley is Mrs. Paley."

"What do you mean?" I asked.

"In the doll corner."

There was Stanley, with the same spiral notebook you use, listening to the girls while they tried on dresses, and scribbling a "story." Then he crawled under the sand table and continued writing. What was the story in his mind? We'll never know. This is one of your mysteries, I guess.

DEAR ANNIE:

Stanley is a subtle character. Perhaps the best way to find out what he has in mind is to ask Marianne. She follows his meaning as clearly as she does Eli's. Your Stanley story makes me even more eager to return to your classroom, but first I must travel to South Carolina and to London for more storytelling and story acting.

Meanwhile, I had the opportunity last week to describe Eli's hurricane drama and your response at a conference of preschool and kindergarten teachers. There were those who were puzzled by your "calm acceptance of chaos" (as one teacher put it). "I enjoyed the Katrina story," she made clear, "but I'd have stopped the play long before Mrs. Olson did. And I wouldn't have been so good-natured about the mess, either. Probably I'd be the jailer, not the National Guard."

We soon found ourselves trying to differentiate between good play and bad play. "How do we know when the play is working?" someone asked, and then gave her own answer. "When the children are doing something together, quietly and cooperatively, I say the play is good. But when the explosions begin I am ready to pounce, even before I hear any explanations."

At this point I told my Emily anecdote, and the "bad stuff, bad stuff" reminded one of the preschool teachers of a similar occurrence in her classroom. A boy kept calling children "bad dog, bad dog" and pushing down their blocks and Lego constructions. It turned out that this little boy had a puppy at home who was constantly being yelled at and punished. Apparently it upset the boy more than anyone realized. "So here he was," the teacher told us, "trying to make a scene out of a family crisis and I saw it simply as bad play."

"That's it!" another teacher called out. "He was making a scene. This must be the way Mrs. Olson judged the hurricane play. It was a scene in a drama. And what she did—what she was prepared to do—was to make up a new scene with the children that worked better in a classroom."

Well, my friend, I'd say these teachers are on to something. They will have had much to think about when they returned to their classrooms.

11 ∗ more chaos OLD PERSON ON FIRE!

"Stop that, Sam!" a teacher shouts as I walk into a Head Start classroom in South Carolina. She smiles apologetically at me and then repeats her warning. "Sam, I'm not going to tell you again."

Sam, alone in the doll corner, has been twirling a man's tie high in the air. There is no one within reach, but I can understand why it annoys his teacher. Like Emily's fighting dinosaurs, the flying tie does not resemble good play, nor does Sam resemble a boy who is ready to cease his mischief. Suddenly he sees me approaching and, with one more fling through the air, the tie aimed in my direction, he yells out, "Old person on fire!"

Not to be outdone by a four-year-old, I respond, "Old person on fire? That sounds to me like a fireman story. And I happen to be looking for a story to write in my notebook."

Without further instruction, Sam the bothersome twirler of men's ties becomes Sam the storyteller. How could the story appear so fast were it not already in his mind? "The fire truck," Sam begins. "Then the house is on fire. Then an old person. And a cat. And a long hose with strong water. Then I go home."

It sounds like another "boy on the beach" story, but where is the monster in the doll corner? Perhaps that is why he was alone, having earlier identified himself as such.

It is all conjecture and matters not in the present circumstances. We have our opening story and can begin the activity. "Sam told me this story before," I tell the class when we are gathered around the taped stage. "That was when he was twirling a tie in the doll corner."

"It's housekeeping," I am corrected.

"What? Oh, yes, I see we call it by different names. I'll try to remember. Now, about Sam's story. He is the fireman and we'll need someone to be the fire truck, a house, an old person, and a cat. Anyone else, Sam?"

"The strong water."

"Good. We'll all make the sound of strong water when you turn on the hose."

I read Sam's script, and the children perform their parts. They must have known when they saw Sam twirling the tie that he was telling himself a story. Maybe they even wanted to join him then, but the logistics were problematic. The stage is just the right place to solve such structural problems.

Often it is the stories that follow the first one that interest me the most. How do the scenes interact and define these children I have just met? Who will tell the story that somehow brings the others together on common ground? The process is unpredictable, and in this class Eddie will accomplish the feat in a superhero's rescue.

Ellen comes in late, just as we begin to act out Sam's story. She is upset and hangs on to her father. But she is curious about what her classmates are doing with a strange lady, all seated on the floor around a large space fashioned with tape. She rushes over to claim her rights. "My turn!" she calls out, and I explain our purposes. "Sam told me a story, I wrote it down, and we've just acted it out. Would you like to hear it?"

The children and I have taken note of the whispering adults, and no one would deny Ellen her need to be next. She listens to Sam's story and is immediately ready to dictate her own factual report.

"Mommy bumped into a car crash. And the man yelled at her and made her cry. And then we called Daddy and he came to bring me to school."

"Where is Mommy?" I ask.

"She hasta talk to the policeman."

"Shall I put that part in your story?" She nods solemnly, and we begin. It sounds as if we are having a conversation about a serious event. Everyone understands the difference between Sam's twirling tie and the scary accident involving Ellen's mother, another driver, and a policeman. But what Eddie does next reconfirms the idea that children prefer to have their conversations inside a dramatic rendering. Fact and fiction merge to help Ellen and her classmates come to terms with the unexpected and give it a familiar shape. In a quickly told narrative, Eddie connects a doll corner scene with a confusing adult confrontation, and he brings everyone home safely.

"The policeman gives the person a ticket. And the car got on fire. And they put it out with a long hose. And Superman comes to carry them home."

Ellen's father has stayed to watch the story-plays. In a loud stage whisper he tells the teacher, "So, Superman would be me, right? I'm the one who brought Ellen to school, and now I'll go and rescue her mom."

12 * letters

DEAR YU-CHING:

Do you see the Emily anecdote I sent you as a love story? If Blanc, the "you are beautiful" boy, is involved in love stories, how do Emily's fighting dinosaurs qualify?

DEAR VIVIAN:

Yes, even Emily is practicing friendship. Her mother's way is anti-friendship and anti-love. The way she sees it, someone is not your friend if they eat at McDonald's. She gives her daughter no way to make a friend. So Emily figures it out herself. She invents a kid dinosaur and a baby dinosaur who fight but also dance and fly together; in other words, they are trying to play with each other. She shows that they have become friends when she herself becomes the one who eats the "bad stuff." She has stepped into the other child's shoes. In Chinese folklore that is called friendship.

By the way, Blanc is continuing to practice friendship with Yu-shan. He has gone as far as he could calling her beautiful and making her his baby bear, so now he puts her into a number of other books we read.

In that wonderful book Wen-Fong sent you, On My Way to Buy Eggs, by Chih-Yuan Chen, Blanc copies the girl in the book and says, "I'm a little fish, swimming in the big blue sea." He puts a blue tissue paper over his face and gives one to Yu-shan. She must be a little duck swimming with him. But Yu-shan answers, "I'm the blue cat who goes to buy eggs, and you can be the fish." Yu-shan knows that in true friendship stories, each friend has an equal say.

DEAR YU-CHING:

Let me get back to the idea of creative kindness. Finding a new way of being a friend is the supreme act of kindness. It is important to keep the door open. Emily's mother closed the door, but Emily's story will help to open it up again. The anecdote demonstrates how subtle the play of children can be. This is one reason we must closely watch, listen, and write it down verbatim.

Sometimes, of course, the connections are simple and obvious. Take, for example, this scene in a Chicago daycare center. A small boy has been sent to a time-out chair, isolated from the other children. I don't know what the offense has been, but he is on the verge of tears and stares down at the floor.

Across the room, an even smaller girl has been watching him while she draws rainbows on a large paper. She sits on the floor and uses the biggest size hollow block as her table. When her picture is finished, she signs her name with the letters "A" and "S," puts away the crayons, and then begins to push the hollow block toward the boy.

It is hard work. She keeps dropping the picture, picking

it up, pushing the block, and dropping the picture again. Finally she reaches the boy's side and sits next to him, on the block. "I made you a picture," she says. "You can hold it."

The boy shakes his head and turns away. A few more minutes go by and then the little girl asks, "Do you want to be Batman?"

A flicker of a smile appears. "I'm Robin," he tells her. "You can be Wonder Woman." Instantly, everything about these two children has changed. You can see the relief on their faces. "Pretend I'm trying to find you," the boy says, "and I don't know you're in the Batmobile." Softly he starts up the motor of the Batmobile and the two children leave the classroom behind. Is this not a love story?

13 : moving rocks

Before I can revisit those scenes of hurricanes, howling wolves, and butterfly sisters in Mrs. Olson's kindergarten, I travel to the Borough of Brent in northwest London, to talk to schoolteachers about play and collect more stories from young children.

This is in a neighborhood of great integration of people, cultures, and languages, in the shadow of Wembley soccer stadium. The people passing me on the street as I leave the Underground are likely to be speaking Bengali, Somali, Farsi, Gujarati, Urdu, Arabic, and Albanian. The Borough of Brent is home to many refugees, asylum seekers, and economic migrants. Their children go to the neighborhood schools together and, as I will soon discover, tell stories similar to those I have heard in my own classes. If anything, the unusual circumstances in which they are being asked to tell a story makes them more intent upon connecting their voices in a communal narrative. They begin with what they saw on their walk to the conference site and end with magic rocks and wondrous families looking for stability and belonging. Yuching would, I think, accept these as friendship stories.

Twenty children from two nearby preschools have been walked over to help me demonstrate the storytelling and story acting method I've been using in my classroom for many years. The audience is made up of several hundred preschool teachers, college teachers, and student teachers. They are all surprised at how quickly the children understand what it is I want them to do.

"Are we real or pretend?" a little girl asks in a clipped British accent. I laugh at myself: *I* am the one with the accent, not the child.

"Either one," I say. "We'll do this story first and you can see how it works. I need a butterfly and a flower. 'The butterfly is on the flower. It sniffs the flower and then it flies away.'"

The moment the children watch the story acted out, several arms shoot up. "Can I do a butterfly one too?" a girl named Jesse asks. "But mine has a bush too. And a rock. And a flower. And she flies over the flower and the bush and the rock and another flower and another flower. We saw this really on our walk." Thus we begin with the "real" and make our way quickly into the pretend. As soon as the things on Jesse's list of items seen on the walk are recreated as actors on a stage they become authentically pretend, and they seem to reach out to one another as friends.

Shayda is next. "A butterfly. She flies to a rock. The rock moved. And it moved again. Then the rock and the butterfly come to a flower. They find their family. And they have raindrops for supper."

Now we are in doll corner territory. "Who is the family, Shayda?" I ask, and she tells us, "The butterfly and the rock and the flower is a family." Most of the children seem to find this a satisfying arrangement, but Adita waves an arm and stands up.

His story has a strongly masculine flavor, but it retains the butterfly as a character. "When the rock is zooming away, he carries the butterfly on his back. The rock is strong. He crashes into another rock. And then I jump on the roof of the house."

"You are the rock that is zooming away?"

"Yes. And then I jump off."

"Off the roof?"

"Yes. And I'm still carrying the butterfly. Unharmed. Un*harmed*." This must be a new word he has learned. Some of the children say it with him, and they grin at each other, as if suddenly realizing that they are allowed to inject *harm* into a story.

However, the next two storytellers are girls whose stories contain no harmful effects. Tarrenay settles her characters into a garden. "Once upon a time," she begins and then pauses. She is a small dark child with ribboned braids all over her head. "It's good, once upon a time?" I nod and she continues. "And there was a butterfly and a rock in the garden. And a flower. The butterfly comes to the flower because the flower is the mother. And a bee flies to the mother, to make a buzzing sound. And the rock is the father. The butterfly is the baby and the bee is the sister."

Sansa, the boy sitting beside her, asks, "Is that the bee we saw when we walked here? That one is in my story too. It flies into the butterfly. And he says I'm sorry. And they sit on the rock and he carries them high up and higher and higher until no one can see them."

"Is that my rock?" Adita wants to know. Sansa was a rock in Adita's story. "Not the one that's zooming," he clarifies, which annoys Amalia. "Why does the rocks all the time moving? Rocks can't move by theirself!"

"Yes, if you throw a rock. Or crash into a rock," Adita argues.

"Well, not in my story," Amalia states. "Only moving things move. Once there is a flower in the ground. And a rock. It does not move. It is staying. The butterfly stops. Only the rain is moving. And the cold is coming down. And the butterfly and the flower and the rock looks at the rain. No one is moving. Only the rain."

John tells the final story. "The rock is magic. So it flies everywhere. And it goes to school every day. And it plays in the park. I am the rock." John is the only actor in his story, and several children mention this. We all watch him intently as he flies around the stage, goes to school, and plays in the park. Amalia nods in approval. "If it's magic, the rock can move," she says.

It was a cold, rainy day in London. But inside the conference hall there are warm feelings we are eager to examine. How is it that these youngsters are so forthcoming and so willing to make such generous connections to each other's stories in front of a large audience of strangers?

After the children leave the hall to walk back to their

schools, the teachers and I talk about what we have just seen and heard. "The smoothness of the performance amazed me," one teacher says. "With a brief demonstration they understood everything. I would have thought more preparation is necessary."

"But isn't that the point?" A woman stands in the row behind the first speaker. "This activity is just like play and they already know how to play. You weren't teaching them something. You were, in a sense, letting them play in a garden and make up stories with butterflies, flowers, crashing rocks, and magic."

"It's not so simple," another teacher calls out. "If these kids had been just told to play in any way they wished, there would have been no such response. Even on the playground, children are left out and wander around. This is a safer experience. You taped an enclosure, inside of which everyone had the same right to play. Even the boy at the end who acted out a story by himself was not alone. The others watched him, imagining every step of the way. What comes across to me is this: Loneliness is impossible in this activity."

There is a hush in the hall. The statement about loneliness catches us all by surprise, and I repeat the final speaker's words. "Loneliness is impossible in this activity." This seems a good place to end the session. Could anything be more important to think about in a preschool classroom than loneliness? How does one learn to be someone who is not lonely? "The butterfly and the rock and the flower is a family." This must surely be part of the way children learn not to be lonely.

14 ∶ the ocean and the island

"Hey, Stan! Stanley! Come on, you gotta see this!" Eli's shouts to Stanley are the first words I hear as I enter Mrs. Olson's room after a two-month absence. The idea that Stanley is now being summoned into the block area comes as a surprise; his effect on block play usually caused some anxiety among his classmates. Stanley, however, does not respond. He is busy crouching under the sand table, almost hidden from sight.

I have no trouble locating him. His growls and cries are remarkably penetrating, even during a noisy playtime. He pushes two wooden animals, one in each hand, sliding them across the sandy floor. The plan is simple: going forward they make straight tracks and on the return they zigzag a trail of Xs. After a moment he brushes away the lines and begins the pattern again. Is his play so different from Eli's at the beach? And yet I do not ask Stanley about his animals as I freely asked Eli about his sand house. The unspoken message Stanley sends to me is "keep away." This may reflect my own attitude more than his, but I do not approach.

By contrast, Eli and the boys he builds with are carrying on a public drama. They are inviting everyone's attention. "Hey, Paulie, look at this! Anthony, come see what we got!"

Eli, George, and Mark have constructed a multilevel garage next to a large blue plastic sheet. "This is the ocean and this is the island," they inform all who pass by. "Don't touch anything. This is the ocean and this is the island."

Several children come to watch, and a few linger, waiting for something to happen. Stanley's arrangement under the sand table seems far more interesting to me, but except for an occasional glance from Mrs. Olson, no one seems to notice. The main attraction is on the rug. "This is the ocean and this is the island" has now been announced six times since I walked in, and if anything the general interest is increasing.

Raymond puts a small Lego car on the edge of the plastic sheet, ready to drive it into the garage.

"Hey, watch out!" Eli yells gruffly. "You wanna blow up the ocean?"

Raymond is offended. "It was a accident. Anyway, oceans don't blow up. Water can't explode."

"Oh, yeah? Oh, yeah?" Eli gives him a squinty-eyed look and brings out a small boat. "This boat explodes water. It sucks up waves."

"Yeah? Well, I got a Mobile X-0007 with titanium hardware. I'm exploding your boat, Eli." The boys have found their story, and the words pour out so fast I can barely write them down or even identify the speakers.

"If I touch your boat you die!"

"Calling X-0007! Do you read me?"

"Blow it to smithereens! The wall is coming down!"

"Blow it up! The boat is sinking!"

"The island is sinking. Watch out for the ocean!"

The sound of the bell catches the boys by surprise. They seem puzzled as they stare at the island and the ocean. Everything is as before. The action has been imagined and verbalized, but the physical representation of the words still has not taken place.

"Are we having another play time, Mrs. Olson?" Eli pleads. "We didn't do the ocean and the island yet."

"But I heard you do it," Mrs. Olson insists. "Everyone within a mile heard you."

"Not the real explosion! And not the drowning we didn't." Eli is distraught. "Can't we save this?"

"I'm sorry," Mrs. Olson says, kindly. "We'll need the whole rug for our math lesson. Maybe you can build it again after lunch, if there's time." She has already turned her attention to Stanley, who is now completely out of sight.

"Come out, Stanley, please? Carrie has to sweep up the sand. You have your job too, you know." His back is to the teacher, and he continues to move his animals.

Mrs. Olson whispers something to Marianne, who kneels down and touches Stanley's arm. "I need you to be Grandpa. Okay, Stanley?"

Without looking up, Stanley puts the animals in a shoebox that has his name on the top and on the sides and crawls out from under the table, pushing the box ahead of him. He places the box on a nearby windowsill that also has his name prominently displayed. "Okay, Stan?" Marianne takes his hand. "I gotta hang up the dresses, and you can put away the dishes, okay?"

Stanley seats himself on the rocking chair and surveys the cleanup chores going on around him. Then, in a soft, clear voice, he sings, "The ocean and the island, the ocean and the island, this is the ocean and this is the island." Soon, everyone in the doll corner is singing along with him as they complete their jobs.

After school, Mrs. Olson and I have our tea at the story table. "Do you think Stanley will ever dictate a story to us?" she asks, passing the cookie tin.

"I've been wondering about that too, Annie. What if I had said to him before, 'Can I write down your story about the animals making Xs in the sand'?"

"I've tried that, you know, several times. But I got nowhere. It was as if he didn't hear me. And once he actually brought his animals to the story table and sat for a while, moving them back and forth. But when I asked if he'd like to be on the story list, he just closed his eyes."

"Well, we know he listens to the children's play," I point out. "You heard him before, didn't you, repeating Eli's ocean and island mantra? That was the first time I'd heard Stanley make use of another child's imagery."

"Marianne can get him to do that," Mrs. Olson tells me. "He trusts her. But don't you have the feeling he's on the verge of doing a story for us, somehow?"

"Yes, I do. Maybe a 'Stanley the wolf' story?" We

both laugh as we refill our teacups. "Of course, there's no knowing in advance what character a child wants to be, but I'm certain that Stanley needs this sort of structure to go public one day."

I began my experience in Annie Olson's kindergarten watching Eli and Marianne, confident children who are at ease in the practice of being a child. But my thoughts now revolve around Stanley, whose practice in the matter is far less understood. And yet the girls did not copy Eli's "the ocean and the island" chant. Instead they waited for Stanley to reinterpret the event and followed his lead.

Driving home, a line from the Psalms comes to mind: "The stone which the builders rejected has now become the cornerstone."

15 ⁝ letters

DEAR YU-CHING:

You remember I told you about Stanley, a boy in Annie Olson's kindergarten? He is quite different from the others, and I'm sure has some worrisome labels attached to his name. But the children like him, even though he can be disruptive and inaccessible. He knocks down buildings, barely noticing what he has done, and he seldom responds to those who call his name or ask him a question.

The thing is, the children do call his name and ask him questions. They are curious about him even when he appears to ignore them. Yesterday an amazing thing happened, a real event. Stanley picked up a phrase that Eli had been repeating in his block play with two other boys. Then, during cleanup, sitting in the doll corner, Stanley began to sing out Eli's exact words, and everyone around him joined in. You could see that the children knew something important was going on.

Now his teacher and I are wondering when Stanley will tell his first story for us to act out. And who will he choose to be? The children say he is a wolf when he growls, and Marianne calls him "Grandfather" when he sits in the doll

corner rocking chair. But mainly he likes to sit alone under
the sand table and play with his animals.

DEAR VIVIAN:

Two children you've written about remind me of Stanley.
There was Jason, who flew into every child's story, drown-
ing out their words with his helicopter roar. And there was
Simon, who also broke into other children's stories and
played alone under a table with little animals. One day he
brought his animals to the stage and seemed to be telling
them a story. "Walk, walk, walk," he said to each one, and
the children began to copy him.

As I see it, Stanley is looking for a way to tell his story,
in other words, to become more necessary to the group. He
tries out something Eli said to see if it works for him. By the
way, what was the phrase he copied?

DEAR YU-CHING:

Out of context, I'm afraid Eli's words won't make sense,
but here they are: "The ocean and the island." Importantly,
these words captured the attention of a number of children
including Stanley, who at the time was hidden under the
table with his animals. Apparently his imagination was
stimulated in the same way as the other children, and none
of us knew it. So he let us know it. As I said, this was a real
event in the life of Annie Olson's classroom.

16 : almost a day at the beach

The day after our conversation, when Stanley is taken out of class by the special education teacher, Mrs. Olson gathers the children together on the rug for a promised discussion about the story list. Some children want to be able to sign up in advance for the next day's list. According to the present rule, the only names put on that list are those who weren't called the previous day because the time ran out.

"We shouldn't really have this discussion yet," Mrs. Olson says, looking around. "I just realized that Stanley isn't here. Mrs. Jackson took him out. He might want to hear all your opinions and maybe give his own."

"He doesn't sign his name on the list," Julia says. "I don't think he does."

"You're right, Julia. So far, Stanley hasn't dictated a story for us to act out." Mrs. Olson holds up the story list. "If I sign his name on tomorrow's list, do you think he'll want to tell a story?"

Eli has immediate doubts. "He doesn't want you to do that. He can write his own name. You have to wait until tomorrow and ask him."

"If he did tell us a story," Mrs. Olson persists, "I wonder what it would be about."

There is universal agreement. "A wolf!" everyone calls out together. Marianne goes further in imagining the script. "The wolf growls. That's his story. And he lives in a cave."

"Maybe he'll want to be a grandfather, Marianne. In the doll corner you sometimes call him Grandfather."

"Yeah, that's just what I call him," she says, "when I don't want him to growl."

"If Stanley does tell a wolf story, will there be anyone else in his story? Eli, what do you think?"

"No one else. Stanley likes to be a wolf by his own self."

"Okay," Mrs. Olson says. "When Stanley comes back, I'm going to tell him about our conversation. But I'll do it in a different way. You'll see."

After lunch, the children come together again. This time Stanley is part of the group, though he sits on the edge of the rug with his back to Mrs. Olson. "Once upon a time," she begins, "there was a boy who pretended to be a wolf. He liked to growl and sometimes to pounce. But mostly he walked all around until he found his favorite farm animals. 'Let's make *X*s in the sand,' the wolf said. So the wolf and the cow and the sheep walked together and made *X*s in the sand."

Mrs. Olson directs everyone to take places around the rug in order to act out her story. "George, will you be the wolf? And Sybil and Jenny, the cow and the sheep?"

Stanley has not moved from his spot on the edge of the rug, but he turns to watch as Mrs. Olson repeats the script and the actors perform their roles. The wolf growls, the cow moos, the sheep goes baa, and all the animals make Xs on the rug. Then the children do something quite spontaneously that is not in the teacher's script. They pretend to erase the Xs, make them again, erase them again, and make them a final time. It is the way Stanley does his own story under the table, and everyone is familiar with the routine. It has now become as public as "the ocean and the island."

Mrs. Olson stands up. "Well, shall we all go outside and play? We've been sitting too long." A good story-teller knows when to stop the narrative and move on. The story can continue on its own now, passing from child to child, and always with a little help from their teachers.

It is not quite a day at the beach, but there are all these unexpected miracles along the way when we and the children pause and say, "Life stand still here. We want to watch the scene a while longer."

17 ∗ we together have
a friendship

There are scenes from the past that I would like to think about a while longer. The anecdotal history of one group of children suddenly brings to mind other extraordinary characters who changed my perceptions of life in a classroom.

Stanley reminds me of a boy named Dylan who practiced being a child in his own particular way but had the advantage of being in a kindergarten with two even more unusual children. His story cannot be told without theirs, and all these stories pass before me as if they are just happening.

Dylan, Mary Ellen, and Serena are very different from the other children in my kindergarten this year, and from each other as well. They share three characteristics: a deep distrust of teacher-led activities, a degree of self-absorption beyond the norm, and a varying inability to speak in familiar ways in ordinary circumstances.

Dylan, to begin with, is the youngest child of college

professors. At five he has not mastered a language or appropriate social behaviors. "Me'en tiger," he mumbles, pouncing on Shelly, who sits quietly listening to the book I am reading to the group. "Me'en fox," he adds for good measure as he slinks away.

"Stop it, Dylan, I'm telling!" she snaps, and he calls back, "Her deader." He barely notices Mary Ellen scowling at him from the edge of the rug. "Who cares?" she hisses when he passes close enough to touch. "I isn't listening to you." Nor is she listening to me.

Mary Ellen rises to her feet as if in a dream and sashays around the rug, mimicking images none of us recognize. She stops when she approaches Serena, the third member of this wandering trio who always leave the group whenever a book is being read.

Serena is busy writing at a corner table. She knows how to read and write but takes little pleasure in books or in people. Even so, it is to Serena that Mary Ellen has confided, "My mommy and daddy doesn't live with me no more." She has been sexually abused and now lives with her grandmother. Her grammar poses no problem, but she cannot keep unwanted memories out of her sentences for long when she plays, mainly in the form of a wolf who calls her his "girlfriend." Dylan is especially drawn to Mary Ellen's imagery and frequently offers himself as Fox, ready to eat the wolf. Serena calls the wolf a "not-wolf," which surprises no one, since she often speaks to us in coded messages.

Right now, as I read to the class, Serena is printing words on squares of colored paper. Her thoughts are sometimes expressed in lists and categories that she invents each day. Her parents, who own a restaurant, were proud of their daughter's early accomplishments but are now concerned about the odd uses to which she puts her talents.

Before lunch, Serena passes out her neatly printed cards. They read: "NOT LIBBY," "NOT ADRIANNE," "NOT PETER," and include everyone in the class. We have all been alphabetized and organized by color into nonpersons. A–E is on red, F–J is on pink, K–O is on white, P–T is on blue, and U–Z is on yellow. "R is absent," she writes, since we have no names beginning with R. She does this also for Q and Z.

The children scratch out "NOT" when they discover what the cards say, and Serena screams, "Don't do that!" Her eyes fill with tears. "Tell them not to!" she demands of me. When I explain that the children don't want to be a "NOT," she is genuinely surprised. "Why don't they?" she asks. Dylan and Mary Ellen are the only ones who seem pleased with their cards, a fact I point out to Serena, who then asks, predictably, "Why do they?"

It is tempting to label and classify Serena, Mary Ellen, and Dylan, as Serena does to us, but none of the categories I might choose has anything to say about the stories they dictate for us to act out. All three, so quick to misconstrue the meaning of ordinary events, are in fact passionate and, for the most part, sensible storytellers. Later in the year, Serena will understand that if she puts such ideas as her nonperson cards into a drama—a dictated story to be acted out—the children will happily accept their roles. Similarly, Dylan's fox and tiger, and even Mary Ellen's wolf, if contained in a script, lose their power to offend or frighten when presented as characters in a story. "Even Mary Ellen's wolf," I say, but the wolf lost his power when she was finally able to keep him *out* of her story.

The logistics of storytelling and acting appealed to all three children almost immediately. Serena, with her fondness for lists, grabs the story list on the day it is introduced and enters her name on three separate lines. The next day she "steals" the list and rewrites the column of names so that hers is at the top. The children object, of course, although they enjoy telling me, "Serena is stealing the list!" Interestingly, her fascination with the story list increases nearly everyone's desire to be on it. One day she rewrites the list so that the first and last letters of each name are omitted and put into the name below. She continually changes these letters until, ten rows later, the original names appear again.

The story list quickly becomes our most publicized collection of names. Everyone learns to read every other child's name from the story list, a sensible reaction to the question, often posed, "Who's doing a story today?" Dylan finally begins to write his name in order to be included on the list. Mary Ellen, who prints her name beautifully but refuses to mark any of her possessions with her name or even post it on her cubby, makes certain it is on the story list before she hangs up her coat in the morning. Most important, these three children carry on their most persistent conversations, with each other and with other children, at the story table. They sit there now awaiting their turns.

Mary Ellen is poised to speak. Hers is usually the most difficult story for me to write down because she begins by inserting material she does not want. She must rid herself of the "bad stuff" if the good story is to emerge. "Once upon a time," she says, "there was a little puppy. And then the huge big wolf says—no, he's not in it!—just me, no wolf!"

"Red little riding girl?" Dylan asks.

"No, it's not. You don't know!" She looks annoyed but Dylan knows she likes his questions.

"Fox in it, Mary Ellen?"

"No fox, Dylan. He don't know what I'm talking about. Then the wolf says, do you want to be my girlfriend? No, don't say that! That's not in my story."

Serena gives Mary Ellen a card that reads, "NOT WOLF," but then takes it back and erases the word "wolf." The subject has perhaps become too complicated, but all the attention being given helps Mary Ellen settle into the story she wants to tell.

"One time there was a little puppy. Oh, yes. And I'm a little girl. And there is a kitty and me. I'm a princess. I'm so lovely. Love-ly."

"Love-ly," Dylan echoes. "Mousie too?"

"Yeah, there *is* a mousie. We, let us have a we to have three pets. So we together have a friendship. We together saw a rainbow. Lovely, we say lovely. We want a rainbow in the sky. Then Mama says, 'We don't have no time, honey.'"

Serena leans over and puts her finger on "honey." "Honey, Mary Ellen," she says, and then reads the entire story out loud, probably to determine which words were erased. In her own stories there must be no extra spaces between letters or words, and no smudges or unintended dots, "ands," or "buts." She anxiously monitors her own scripts, looking for mistakes, but she wants her stories to be acted out. Her lists are private; her stories provide her with a pathway into the social group and a connection to the teacher. She could easily write her own stories, but she insists on dictating them to me or to the assistant teacher.

Her turn is next. "Once upon a time there was a yellow jacket," she begins. "And it stung everything it saw. And one time it accidentally stung a building. And then a little kid came along and it accidentally stung the little kid. And then the yellow jacket stung almost everything in the whole world. And then the mommy and daddy came and they all got lost with the little kid. And they lived happily ever after."

"Sting fox?" Dylan asks. He knows that Serena never changes or adds a word to her story; it is his little joke, and Serena rewards him with a smile, a rare event. However, Lisa raises a larger issue. "They can't be happily ever after," she argues. Lisa's logic governs our common understanding of such matters, found in all the books we read. But Serena stares at her, uncomprehending.

As if to prove her point, Lisa tells a story in which only good things happen. "Once upon a time there was a little house waiting for people to move inside. And they moved in. And the little house was happy. Then the parents had a little girl and a brother. And they bought a pet rabbit and the pet rabbit had babies. The parents let the children take them for a walk. And they feeded them. And they all lived happily ever after."

Lisa's story is as uncomplicated as she herself seems to be. There are no stinging yellow jackets, no wolves who want little girls for girlfriends, and families are not lost forever. Yet when we act out Serena's story, Lisa begs to be the yellow jacket, flying around stinging everyone. Indeed, this role is so much in demand that we must do repeat performances with multiple yellow jackets. Serena doesn't mind, since she usually leaves the group when her story is being acted out.

I am curious about Lisa's apparent contradictions. "Why do you so much want to be the yellow jacket?" I ask her. "Because it's fun to sting people," she answers. "I think it's very fun."

"Don't sting me," Mary Ellen orders, whereupon Lisa asks everyone to raise their hands if they want to be stung. This, of course, totally changes the intent of Serena's story. No wonder Serena has left the group. She is at the little corner table she likes, compiling another of her secret lists. She allows Dylan to sit beside her, and he knows he must not touch her notebook. He has his "NOT DYLAN" card with him, which he pretends is a car racing around the table. Each time it reaches Serena's arm the card bumps into her, and Dylan whispers "accidentally." He practices repeating Serena's words with great solemnity.

When it is Dylan's turn to tell a story, he warns Serena that there is only one character. "Only me, Serena. Only Fox, only that." He is preparing her for what he knows she will do: run into the hallway and sit on the bench. Serena panics when a story has only one character. She has made a number of compromises for the sake of storytelling, but she cannot accept a one-character story any more than an empty space on a line or an unfinished sentence at the bottom of a page. An extra chair at her lunch table must be explained or removed if she is to remain.

Dylan's story is brief, so Serena does not stay away long. "Then come Fox. That me. Gr-r-r. Jumping and big teeth like this!" When he dictates his story, I ask him if he'd like to add another character. "So Serena can stay with us." He shakes his head, but later in the year he and all the others will avoid one-character stories and, for her part, Serena will agree to act in more stories.

In her own stories, Serena tests herself by reducing the number of characters to two, though she generally likes five characters. Mary Ellen understands that a struggle is taking place. "You almost down to one, Serena," she says, when Serena tells a simple story in which a big kid opens a door for a little kid and then the little kid shuts the door for the big kid. "You almost got one kid!" she exclaims proudly.

Mary Ellen has her own battles. "Once upon a time we was really scary," she dictates one day. "We was pimples and everything. We was so frightening we don't know what to do. The people was so scared of my separation. And then you say kiss, kiss, give me a kiss." This time she doesn't ask me to erase anything, and when we act out her story, the actors huddle together pretending to be frightened. "We was scary, we was pimples and everything" becomes the mantra whenever there is a scary part in a story. This year, the most often quoted sentence is another one of Mary Ellen's: "We together have a friendship." I print it on a sign above the piano, and everyone learns to read her words.

It is Serena, however, who gives us the best prized and most often repeated story of all, which becomes known as the "number 5" story. Somehow it helped explain Serena to us.

"Once upon a time there was a school of kids but there were only five kids in the school. Number 1 liked to jump, number 2 liked to play, number 3 liked to build, number 4 liked to draw, and number 5 was the leader. One day number 5 was the leader, but the teacher said number 1 couldn't jump. And number 5 told number 2 not to play. And then when he was getting the milk, he told number 3 not to build, and when number 5 was going to music, the teacher told number 4 not to draw. And number 5 was the only lucky one that day."

"Do numbers 1, 2, 3, and 4 ever get to be leaders?" I ask Serena.

"No," she answers.

"Only you, Serena?" Mary Ellen asks. "Because it's your story?"

"Number 5 Serena," Dylan states, counting his fingers. "Serena number 5."

Now Serena does something quite remarkable. She walks to the crayon table and prints three words on a card, then hands it to Dylan. "IS NUMBER 5," she reads, pointing to each word. "You have to say *is*, Dylan. You have to say Serena *is* number 5."

"Okay," he nods. "Is number 5, is number 5." He holds the card high above his head and then, unaccountably, begins to run around the room, shouting, "Fox is here, Fox is here!" He leaps into the doll corner, overturns the crib and doll, then stops himself in midair, it seems. Calmly he comes to the story table and points to his name on the list. "Fox is here," he tells me, grinning. "My turn *is* now."

Come to think of it, Dylan and Stanley are not that similar but for the fact that each boy takes comfort in pretending to be a wild animal. With Stanley the behavior is almost unconsciously arrived at, whereas Dylan's purposes seem intended to disrupt and dismay. Oddly enough, both children, with their growls and roars, along with the less threatening meowing kittens, barking dogs, and buzzing bees, somehow humanize the classroom. Clearly, children hear the sounds in a classroom differently than we do.

18 ⁑ stanley's fish

Stanley seems different today. It takes me a few minutes to realize that he is holding a book as he swings around the room and another moment to identify the book as *Swimmy*. This is Leo Lionni's story of the brave little black fish who saves a school of tiny red fish from a giant tuna by teaching them to swim in formation. I remember one class of kindergartners repeating Swimmy's words whenever we lined up to go anywhere. "I have it!" they would shout as Swimmy does. "We're going to swim all together like the biggest fish in the sea!"

Stanley bypasses his usual "cave," as Marianne calls it, and heads for the corner table that houses the fishbowl. He stops to collect his box of animals from the windowsill, then crawls under the table and opens the book to a picture of the giant tuna, mouth open wide, ready to gulp down Swimmy's companions.

"Stanley has a new place to play," I comment to Marianne, who awaits her turn to dictate a story to me.

"Mrs. Olson says you can't bring a library book under the sand table 'cause it's too sandy there," she explains.

"I see that Stanley is reading *Swimmy* to his animals."

"Stanley *is* Swimmy," she says. "Every day."

"Every day? You mean he acts out Swimmy, the way you do with the stories you dictate?"

"No, private. Under the table. Just by his own self."

I continue watching Stanley while Marianne tells a story of three princesses who live in three pink houses next door to one another. Stanley has placed all the wooden animals in a straight line while he turns the pages of the book. Then, one by one, he marches each animal into a space he creates with his stretched out legs. He is definitely Swimmy, and the animals are under his protection.

Mrs. Olson joins me at the story table. "Quite a production, isn't it?" she says. "Do you know what he is saying to the animals? 'Swim all together!' I asked him a few days ago if we could all act out *Swimmy* with him, and he shook his head."

"Shook his head? But that's a new development, isn't it? He's actually responding to you?"

"Right. So I asked him if he minded if we acted out the book without him. This time he didn't respond, but the children weren't eager to do it. Marianne, tell Mrs. Paley what you said."

Marianne is pleased to recall her exact words. "I said it's Stanley's story. He's Swimmy, and he takes out the book all the time."

"That's interesting, Marianne," I comment. "What about your three princesses and three pink houses. Do you mind if someone else tells and acts out your story?"

The answer comes quickly. "No, I don't care. Stanley likes to be more private." That's it. What could be easier to understand? Stanley the wolf aka Swimmy is a more private person.

Later, at my desk, I write a letter to Yu-ching.

DEAR YU-CHING:

Here is an example of creative kindness in which a group shows its friendship by not entering a classmate's story. Stanley has taken Swimmy, the Leo Lionni book, as his own story. He carries the book with him all day and acts it out under the table with his little animals, moving them into place around him as if they are the little red fish who pretend to be a big fish. He himself is Swimmy, the eye of the fish configuration, and he makes them all inch along together.

Mrs. Olson asked Stanley if he would act out his story with the class on a stage, but he refused. Then she asked the children to act out the book without Stanley, and they also refused, saying that it is Stanley's story. He alone is Swimmy.

I think there is an important lesson for us here. The children are happiest when every individual in the group establishes a distinctive persona. They love being able to say that Eli is the hurricane boy, Dylan is Fox, Stanley is Wolf, Blanc is the "you are beautiful" boy, and so on. Is this not the ultimate purpose of play? To identify each individual, as the group is brought together in friendship. "We together have a friendship," Mary Ellen told us in one of her stories, and it became our class motto.

19 : making scenes

"Yesterday was no day at the beach," Mrs. Olson tells me when I arrive early and find her beginning to pack things away. It is the final week of school, and some of the shelves have already been emptied. "Eli was in a horrible mood, and, frankly, I could not conjure up a 'National Guard unit' to help the situation."

"Goodness, what did he do?"

"He was a hurricane minus the plot and the characters. He was disagreeable all day. No one could join him in the blocks; he got into fights with everyone. Nothing would please him. He even cried in the library because a boy in another class took out a book he wanted. He was so miserable with himself and with us that Stanley actually came up to him and handed him another book, one that Eli used to take out months ago."

"Stanley did that? But that's amazing, don't you think? It's as if Eli's difficulties were set up *in order* to give Stanley the opportunity to come forward as a helper. What a great scene!"

My friend Annie looks at me as if I've lost my sanity. "Sorry, Vivian, but I was more inclined by then to lower the curtain and go home. But you know, you're right. Stanley sympathized with Eli more than I did. I guess you could say they exchanged roles; this time Eli was the wolf and Stanley was the good guy."

"Annie, remember when Eli told us that everyone thinks the wolf is mean but really he's not? That, in fact, everyone has to stop thinking the wolf is mean and act nicer to him? Well, yesterday Stanley was the one who made the formula work: when someone is growling and wolfish, you have to act nicer to that person."

Annie pulls a journal out of her desk drawer and turns the first few pages. "Quote," she says, "'Don't talk no more about this. 'Cause Stanley isn't here and he'll want to hear this conversation. He's our friend.'"

Before lunch, when the children are seated on the piano rug, Mrs. Olson says, "I'd like us to talk about summer vacation, which will begin soon. But first, something happened in the library yesterday that I'll remember during the summer. When Stanley saw that Eli was sad because the book he wanted was gone, Stanley brought him a book that used to be his favorite. That was kind of you, Stanley."

"I got a thing to remember too!" Eli calls out. "Remember when we were doing that big hurricane? That was so much fun!" He looks at Stanley. "You weren't here on that day. And we forgot to tell you about the hurricane. We pretended the whole of everybody was drowning and we sat on the roof and got into boats to save us and the wolf was in the boat too. Remember?"

The children do remember. They gaze around the room in silent wonder at the chaotic scenes Eli has brought to mind. "The wolf was howling," Marianne says wistfully. "And I put a blanket over him 'cause he was scared, and Mrs. Olson put on boots and then we all put them on." She turns to Stanley. "And we didn't tell you about how we were the National Guard."

"It's okay," Mrs. Olson says. "You're telling him the whole story now."

"Yeah, yeah," Eli adds. "Because we're friends of everybody in the story and now Stanley's in the story too."

Eli has answered my question: Why do children play the way they do? "Because we're friends of everybody in the story." And when you tell someone your story, that person enters the story and becomes your friend too.

I will think about these memories as I continue to watch children and collect their stories. I'll also write to Yuching and tell her she is right. The stories *are* mainly about love and friendship, no matter if the wolf is howling or the kittens are meowing. One role is as good as another, so long as you can be inside the story and become necessary to the group.